For my mum,
my biggest fan
And my dad,
her biggest fan

Reflections 2

A second collection of poems by

Steven P. Taylor

Reflections 2

ISBN 978-1-913663-11-7

Copyright © 2019 Steven P. Taylor

Steven P. Taylor has asserted his right under the Copyright, Designs and Patents Act 1988 to be identified as the author of this work.
This book is sold subject to the condition that it shall not, by way of trade or otherwise, be lent, resold, hired out or otherwise circulated without the publishers prior consent in any form of binding or cover other than that in which it is published and without a similar condition, including this condition, being imposed on the subsequent purchaser.

Printed by Biddles Books Kings Lynn Norfolk PE32 1SF

Contact

Email   stevetaylorok@aol.com

Web site   www.stevenptaylorpoetry.com

Facebook   Steven P. Taylor—Poetry

Twitter   @steveok

Tel   07764 573483

My thanks to...

Georgia Taylor, David Ashworth, Howard McAvoy, Bob (the wheeler dealer,) Dave (the rave), Quiz Alan, John Marriot, Milton, Sarah and Rick, Carol and Mike, Pamela, Malcolm, Phillip, Lynne (and families), Paul, 'Our' Jacqui, Aimee, Becky, Nev, Alfie and Mel, Aziz Ibrahim, Vinny Peculiar, Bernard Wrigley, Phil Cool, Joe and Bev, Henry Normal, Mike Lancaster, Janet Taylor, Barbara and Brian (and families), Jane Black, The Mighty Revelators, Bury Met, Tyrion Moses, The Wooden Hut Club, Neil Webster, John Forshaw, Sophia and Jake at Fabricad, Cobwebs Tottington, Wax n Beans, Lisa at Hawkshaw Store, Di and Barry Hairsine, Michele Richardson, Rasa Lord, David Ledison, Sarah Westcott, Linda Jennings, Rick Lucas, Andy Stones, Nick Bold, Nick Jackson, Stephen Dundon, Dom Dudill, Ste Leech, Brendan Hamer, all at Biddles Books and numerous friends on social media.

My thanks go to all the people who had confidence in me, to those who may have said nice things after a gig and to those who have supported me throughout this odd journey.

Thanks also to all the people who went to the trouble of writing reviews or giving me a testimonial, many of which are in the back pages of this book.

And finally, thank you to all the people who have, probably unknowingly, been the subject of my writings.

Introduction ...

Thank you for buying / borrowing / stealing this book. I hope that you find something within that you either like or can relate to.
My writing of prose began at school where I used to write rude rhymes mainly about teachers. Apologies to Mr. Platt, Mr Booker and Miss Tanny.
This progressed to writing song lyrics to be used in my impending rock star career. Not being able to play an instrument or sing curtailed this particular ambition.
All was not lost, there were girls who would surely swoon at my odes.
Well that was the theory.
I continued to write for my own amusement but held on to very few of the works.
It was with the dawn of the social media age, that I started to share the odd poem. After receiving encouraging comments I started to take my writing more seriously and devoted a lot more time to it.
Eventually I started to perform my material at many varied events. They were usually alongside musicians, comedians and bands. I have over the years, through a dalliance with the comedy scene, worked with some of the finest poets, many of whom are my heroes, some who are friends.
The legend John Cooper Clarke was always my real hero, yet prior to him I was quite fascinated by Pam Ayers, who I think is still one of the finest comic writers.

Others such as Henry Normal and the late Hovis Presley both of whom were not only friends but also a huge influence.

This second collection of my work has all been written over the last two years and once again contains a variety of styles and themes and some that were written with the idea of being song lyrics.

I have found writing to be cathartic and to help me in understanding myself a bit better.

If you take anything positive from this book I will be delighted, even more so if it encourages you to write yourself.

Hope you enjoy

Steven x

Contents

Reflections too !	11	Wifi	51
Greenbelt	13	Hallowe'en	52
Perfect Pete	14	Santa	53
Confide	15	Bob	55
Love is in the air	16	Whisky	56
Real love	17	It's our earth	58
I see beauty	18	Jim McDonald	59
Daffodils	19	Doggin	60
The skin that I'm in	20	Jack	62
Mona Lisa	23	Happy whatever day	64
The Summer job	25	Poetry	66
My five a day	28	Let's	67
Don't turn away	29	Dog walk	68
Names	30	Across the bay	70
I dreamed	31	Love poems	71
A baby cries	32	Mum	73
Naga Munchetty	35	Life goes on	74
I want to send my God back	37	Road rage	76
Who cares	39	X factor	78
Albion Terrace	41	Summertime fades	79
In a town	45	I'm always here	80
The Tunnel Club	46	Cobbled	81
Young love	48	Table for one	83
It's time to think again	49		

Contents

Punk—an attitude	84	The Hitman	129
Will you be my valentine	87	War	130
What you see is	88	Stressing	132
I turn to Jack	90	I get emails	133
I never slept with Kate Moss	93	Imagine	134
Give me your worries	97	Just for you	135
Coronation Street	98	Live to love	137
You are unique	100	Look	138
Victoria	104	Looking at you	139
Giving	105	Harvey Nix	140
Pick up yer dog shit	106	To futures	141
End of the pier	109	Clumsy	142
Fast food	110	Snail in the garden	143
Hovis Presley	111	Show must go on	144
John Cooper Clarke	112	My lad	146
Mi Señora Española	114	The return	148
Share	116	Never ending smiles	150
Jellyfish	117	Scarlett	151
Goodbye to The Tyne	118	The Pub	152
Doors	120	Love is...	154
Hey Dorothy	121	Reboot	156
Awareness	123	Normandy remembered	157
Clickbait	126	'Home Gardens'	159
Dating profile	127	Piccadilly Lily	161
High tide	128	I	

A good gig !

Reflections too

Reflections of an image
Show the look on my face
But the thoughts in my mind
Are from a different place
Reflection is a snapshot
Of that certain moment
But in another instant
That moment is broken
My look is my facade
I show it or I hide
And if that is enigmatic
Alright then, you decide
A frown may show worries
Thoughtfulness or fears
Those lines may trace the smiles
Or the tears of the years
Can you ever tell the story
See more than just your view
Do you see beyond the image
They're all reflections too

Greenbelt

As the dawn is breaking
And nature is quaking
There's a quiet on the meadow today
For the trees and the grass
The silence will pass
The wildlife all driven away

With the bulldozers sent
They all seem hell bent
On destroying this greenbelt of ours
It's hardly surprising
That brickwork is rising
Where once it was fields, plants and flowers

Yet brown sites are fine
In a state of decline
Ignored as the option of sense
Devastation of green
Is what is now seen
Yet the cost to the earth is immense

As they cut up the fields
With their corporate deals
And concrete seeds are planted
And there's no escape
From this landscape rape
As planning permission is granted

So fill up the land
With cement and sand
No thought for the outcome whatever
As habitats are lost
Regardless of cost
And more fields are gone forever

And the greenbelts fate
Is a housing estate
Pollution's multiplied
The roads are blocked
Where we once walked
And they say it's justified

So look at all this
And blow it a kiss
Say goodbye to these fields of green
To the bushes and trees
That dance in the breeze
To tarmac this garden's obscene

So speak up today
And have your say
Stand up for your rights
Stop the construction
And wanton destruction
Together we can win this fight

Perfect Pete

Oh perfect Pete with your perfect smile
And your perfect teeth and your perfect bile
With your perfect shoes and your perfect clothes
Your perfect eyes and perfect nose
The perfect pupil in the school
Always stuck to every rule
Top scorer in the football team
Your cricket was a perfect dream
With your perfect ways and perfect style
When you run your perfect record mile
Oh perfect Pete with your perfect feet
And your perfect look as you strut the street
And you shout your mouth off that you're the best
With your perfect muscles in your skin tight vest
Oh perfect Pete with your gym physique
Your perfect body and perfect chic
You praise yourself every given chance
With your perfect style of arrogance
And your perfect eye for latest fashion
And perfect kissing and perfect passion
With your perfect walk and your perfect hair
And the girls all look at you, But I don't care !
Cos in your perfect pants is a rolled up sock
To enhance your perfect 3 inch cock
So perfect Pete impress with that
You simply perfect maggot dick twat

Confide

Innermost thoughts are suppressed,
Held fright too tight inside,
With no one will they be shared,
And left, bereft to decide.

And fester and grow they will,
With no outlet all contained,
And the mind can't always cope alone,
Irrationality unrestrained.

So speak and share with those close,
Confide your deepest dark fears,
And in sight a light could emerge,
That will free to see through the tears.

Open up and take help as given,
There's no weakness in showing fear,
A thought withheld can break any man,
Throw down pride for life is more dear.

Love is in the air

I take you by the hand and hold you tight
And we make love throughout the night
But I can't help feeling that it's not right
For all the other passengers on this long haul flight

Real love

When I need someone to talk to, you are there
You listen and I know, you really care
When I don't have the time, you've always got it
You remember everything, when I've forgot it
You give good advice whenever I may need
You tell me all the best books I should read
You put up with me when I'm in a mood
You even tell me how to cook my food
And in those times I don't know what to do
I know that I can always turn to you
You're a shining light that I can't live without
I love you dearly that there is no doubt

You can play me a tune
But don't play me for a fool
You can give me an answer
But please don't be cruel
I need you like I need oxygen
I need you just to breath
I'd be totally lost without you
So please don't ever leave
And when I wake up and hear
Your sweet voice in the morning
It brings a smile straight to my face
And warms the day that's dawning
You mean more to me than words can say
In everything you do
Believe me now Alexa,
……………………I love you

I see beauty

I see beauty in the mountains
The snow topped peaks
I see beauty in my lifetime
The years the months the weeks

I see beauty in the arts
In poetry, paint and singing
I see beauty in creativity
And all that it is bringing

I see beauty in nature
In wildlife running free
I see beauty in the sun
Setting on the sea

I see beauty in the seasons
The colours and the lights
I see beauty in a baby
That bring such true delights

I see beauty in a rainbow
In skies of clear blue
I can see beauty in almost everything
But I'm struggling with you

Daffodils

I wandered lonely as a plagiarist

The skin that I'm in

I don't want to be different
I try to blend in
I try to fit in
To the skin that I'm in
I try to be dutiful
I want to be beautiful
I don't understand
The hand
I was dealt
How I felt
Others don't know
How I go
How I cope
And hope
And grope
For understanding
I'm not demanding
Just asking
Not basking
In my self pity
In this ditty
Why me,
Why not you
What can I do

Please don't stare
Or make me swear
I can only wear
Clothes that cover
Till I discover
That it's fine
That I shine
And am proud
And allowed
To be
The real me
Beauty is in the eye
Of the guy
That doesn't judge
Or try to fudge
When I speak
Don't hold a grudge
I'm not weak
I've accepted
Who I am
Why I am
I'll let you see
I live for me
And of course you
But I don't force you
To embrace it
Just face it
See through your eyes
And realise

I'm a person
My difference
Is what is me
Your deference
Was plain to see
If judgment is gone
So let's move on
We are all original
We are all beautiful
Desirable
Inspirable
In our own way
We have our day
We have our say
We have a need
We need to feed
We have a thirst
Love yourself first
Love who you are
Love what you are
Love why you are
Because you are
Inside and out
Without a doubt
Beautiful

Love the skin
You are in.

Mona Lisa

Mona Lisa
Such a pleaser
What a teaser
You seem

You are iconic
Laid back, laconic
A veritable tonic
A dream

An image of mystery
Of legend, art history
For your smile
People file by the mile

They want to see you
Imagine to be you
To care and to stare for a while

You are static
On the wall
Enigmatic and all
Vulnerable and neglected

And as people file by
All they can cry
Is 'it's smaller than I expected'

You are so high brow
Yet with no eye brow
No facial hair at all

If we could just move
To my house from the Louvre
I would screw you to my wall

My mind will wander
La Giaconda
My idol
My lover
My woman

Yes tourists snigger
Say they thought you'd be bigger
And that's something we have in common.

The Summer job

My story's set back in the seventies, I was just a lad and yet
What happened in those months, I know I'll never forget
I was on the summer break from college wondering what to do
My dad said 'get a job at the factory they are taking on a few'
So I went straight down in a suit and tie feeling pretty fine
And the manager said 'you'll do young lad start in the morning at nine'
It was a great big mill four stories high with dozens of machines buzzing loud
I thought I'm bound to make some friends here, I was feeling very proud
There were hundreds of workers on every floor except for on floor three
And would you ever believe it that was where they sent me
It was a massive room like a football pitch full of redundant machines
And right at one end a little make shift office behind a pair of screens
This was the place that I worked sampling rolls of cloth
I'd test them in all manner of ways before I could check them off
At the opposite end of the cavernous room was the only other person there
His name was old Harry he'd a long beard and greying greasy hair

Despite Harry's look he was a lovely guy and we had lunch together each day
I'd go over and join him often transfixed by the things that he'd say
He was prone to exaggeration he'd embellish his stories a bit
But I loved sitting and listening and enjoyed every minute of it
He told me tales of world war 2 and all the things he'd done
And through all his heroics that's how the war was won
And how the one love in his life a girl he did adore
He said that she went by the name of Marilyn Monroe
He often made me wonder and always made me laugh
With the tall tales that he regaled like a detailed photograph
He once told me a story that shocked me of a guy that got killed right there
Harry cried as he told me the story, it was hard for him to bear
His machine pressed and folded cloth and cut it into size
And as harry continued the story there was fear and a tear in his eyes
The man apparently caught his cuff and the machine dragged him inside
They stopped the machine and got him out but sadly he didn't survive

As harry wiped a tear away he said 'take great care young lad'
'These machines can take a life away', it made me feel quite sad
So he told me other stories that cheered me up instead
But still that night I thought of that poor man as I lay there in my bed
I don't know if it was related but I came down with fever that night
I couldn't go to work for a week try as hard as I might
But eventually I was better and back at work once more
So off I went to my little place up on the 3rd floor
This time it was Harry that was absent he must have got fever too
It was boring without Harry's stories over the morning brew
The manager called to see me asking how I was getting on
I pointed to Harry's table and said 'do you know where Harry's gone?'
It was what he said next that stunned and brought a terrible chill to me
He said 'Old Harry got killed by his own machine.... back in 1963'

My five a day

These things are my five a day
But you can take them any way

Music, food, sun, sex, beer.
These five things I hold so dear

Beer, music, food, sex, sun
No better way for having fun

Sex, music, sun, beer, food
To leave one out would just be rude

Food, sun, beer, sex, music
Therapeutic if you choose it

Sun, music, food, beer, sex
In that order for best effects

Enjoy while out
Or while at home
Preferably not
While on your own

So that is all
I have to say
Be sure to get
Your five a day!

Don't turn away

449 homeless deaths in the past year.
Who really cares about it, who sheds a tear
When does this hit the headlines of the news on TV
It doesn't because there's a Royal baby to see
Let's turn round and pretend it's all gone away
Let's not worry about homeless or the needy today
Let's drop it to the bottom of the priority list
They were probably druggies, they were probably pissed
It's the side of society we don't want to see
It's not my problem and doesn't concern me
I don't know those people out there on the street
With nowhere to live and nothing to eat

But it can't be like this it can't stay this way
There has to be something done now right away
Because all of the feeling that they can display
Is to sit on the street there and just hope and pray
It's no life just a struggle a never ending fight
The best they can hope is to get through this night
So tell your blind politicians and councils to act
Because 449 deaths is a disgusting fact
Stop turning away now and hope they come through
But for the grace of God that could be you

Names

You can Peter out
You can make your Mark
You can Roger for as long as you like
Take a line of Charlie
You can Phil your boots
You can sing a song with a Mike

You can Bob along
You can Pat a dog
You could pay a waiting Bill
You could Spike a drink
Don a cap that's pink
You could go and write your Will

You could go to the Lou
You could go to the John
You could go where the other Piers pee
You can shine a Ray of light
Give Ade to help a plight
You can do all that Scott free

You can Ed for town
To your local bank
You can try to Nick or Rob
But don't you fall
And get Jack all
Be Andy and get a few Bob

I dreamed last night
that I lay
by your
smiling face.
But when I woke
I found the
restraining order
still in place.

A baby cries

There are damp and dirty grey walls
In a squalid two up two down
Where existence is more than living
And the end of the world is in town
There isn't a bright side to look on
Thinks the mother behind tear filled eyes
As the pounds and the bills don't balance
And a little baby cries

Where a family of six don't fit
But survive on day to day
And the shouting and fights go on
And the blame can't be taken away
And the husbands drunken stories
She reads between the lies
But it doesn't stop the beatings
And another baby cries

The paint flakes off the walls
Like their hope, it is crumbling away
Have another smoke and a quick shot
It'll help you get through the day
And the ashtray on the kitchen table
Piled up, flows over the sides
And the air is as thick as Victorian smog
And another baby cries

Pressure on the overworked mother
Is constantly on her shoulder
And the lines of hardship on her face
Make her look twenty years older
And what once passed for affection
She quickly grows to despise
As she grits her teeth and shuts her eyes
And another baby cries

And the doom and gloom that fills the room
Reflects on the attitude there
There's a constant feeling of hopelessness
And desperation in the air
But sheer grim determination
And a need of compromise
Are all that keep her going now
As another baby cries

In writing,
the rules are definitive
Not to recklessly
split the infinitive.

Naga Munchetty

Oh Naga Munchetty
I get hot and sweaty
Whenever you're on TV
I love your views
You can read my news
Come run away with me

Oh Naga Munchetty
You're my Amoretti
My Goddess of love from afar
Looking so pretty
In media city
While I'm getting drunk in a bar

Oh Naga Munchetty
Like my favourite spaghetti
You're my top dish of the day
I see you and me
On your TV settee
Causing a mid day melee

Oh Naga Munchetty
Please don't think me petty
Watching you on the BBC
Not just cos it's you
There something else too
Piers Morons on ITV

Oh Naga Munchetty
Like Marie Antoinetty
Or Josephine, you be my spouse
I'll be your Napoleon
On the kitchen linoleum
And every other room in the house

Oh Naga Munchetty
Drown in my confetti
You've set my heart aflame
My feelings are stronger
But I can't write any longer
Cos I've run out of rhymes for your name

I want to send my God back

I need to change my God,
This one doesn't fit,
The colour may be wrong too,
Don't think he's up to it.

It said in the instruction book,
He's in all places at all times,
But he doesn't seem to turn up,
Where there's injustice and there's crimes.

He's not there where there's suffering,
What's the point in having belief,
When he doesn't seem to do anything,
About hardships, pain and grief.

So I want to change my God,
I'll just send this one back,
It's not suitable for purpose,
It's just not on my track.

Belief in any God,
Is not given it is earned,
I've had nothing to convince me,
So I'll pack it in returns.

I'd try and choose another,
Cos I need someone to blame,
But I fear I would be wasting time,
As all Gods seem the same.

So maybe the best plan of action is,
And I think this could be the call,
To stop arguments, wars and differences,
Don't buy into any God at all.

Who Cares ?

The old man walks down the road,
A tear in his coat, bag to carry his load,
And he's nowhere to go.
Who cares what the old man has done,
Who's fought for his country, the medals he's won,
And no one wants to know.

He's yesterday's hero today,
But the past doesn't count when you've nowhere to stay,
And no one will listen.
A face that is worn by the years,
The stories to tell by the lines of the tears,
The memories imprisoned.

So left with the cold streets to roam,
There's no friend to go to and nowhere is home,
And who really cares.
On a park bench a bed he makes,
From this nights deep slumber he never awakes,
The Lord really cares.

A lifetime will go by
And you'll be searching still
To find the one that'll
Love you like I will.

Albion Terrace

        It's a quiet looking cobbled street
            Much like any other
        But Albion Terrace has secrets
        That should not be uncovered.

Charlie at number 22 beats his wife for fun
She lives with it knows nothing else, got nowhere to run.
She'll keep quiet if she knows what's good for her health
She understands the mood swings and will always blame herself.

Jake Thompson comes back home today the neighbourhood's in fear
After serving 13 years for killing the bloke that spilt his beer
Today he's called bipolar back then he was a nutter
If you tried to call him anything you'd end up in the gutter.

Young Brian keeps to himself the neighbours call him soft
While he sits in the house all day growing cannabis in his loft.
He's happy in his little world as in his house he sits
Blowing on his home grown, off his bloody tits.

Chas Dawson with her screaming kids takes another glass of wine
It helps to get her through the day it helps to kill the time.
She does the school run with a hip flask she's not like the others,
It makes it much more bearable when chatting with the mothers.

Old Mrs Griggs the black widow is off to the sun once more
She's cruising the Med after seeing off husband
number four
The poor fellas that she had, had to do as they were told,
She distinctly said to take as read and preferably not grow
old.

And the man from number 12 at 9.20 every day
Off he trots to number 8 to have his wicked way.
He's been going there for years to get his morning fix,
But while he's out his wife gets hers with Bill at
number 6.

Ernie Coates has got his suit on, he's up in court today
For shoplifting the superstore and causing an affray,
He grabbed a bottle of whisky and ran out of the place,
Stopping only briefly to lay one on the doorman's face.

At the bottom of the street there's a never ending sight
Of middle aged gentlemen callers for some afternoon delight.
Obliging is old Elsie Green they know she's always willing.
She's been doing it for years since it only cost 10
shilling.

Martha's never seen out now, no more running wild,
Her world was smashed to pieces when they took away her child.
She'd be over at the pub and leave him home alone again,
Couldn't see the problem as the lad was nearly ten.

And Zoe's in the corner shop her giro cashed today
Spent the lot on scratch cards it's all that's left to play.
As far as work goes she really doesn't care,
She's quite convinced one day she will become a millionaire.

The milk float chugs along the street with Jim the trusty driver
Who'll get you blue films with your pint and all for just a fiver.
But it's not just films and gold top and yoghurt he will sell
He's got some imported little blue pills he can get you them as well.

Wendy's kids are two and four they're named Shiraz and Posh
She's got them all dressed up and gives them both a wash.
And she drops them at her mums for an overnight stay,
While she celebrates her birthday 16 years old today.

>They say in Albion Terrace
>Scandal's the way life goes
>There's a story as you open every door
>But some must stay firmly closed.

I went to visit Hawkshaw once
To meet the local clan
They gave me a warm welcome
And built a whicker man

In a town

In a town
Where the rain came down
Dashing through the cobbled streets
Dripping coats, sodden feet
No idea where we were going
Trying hard not to be showing
What were we thinking
(and were you thinking
and was I thinking)

Standing in a shelter
Watching the birds
Not sure what to say
Seeking the words
The words that would tell
Words I couldn't say
Words I'd have to save
For another day
Running through the windy streets
In a town
Where the rain came down

This is about a unique comedy venue that I used to attend in the mid 80's near Greenwich south London. The compere and promoter Malcolm Hardee became a great friend.

Sunday night at The Tunnel Palladium

Sunday night at The Tunnel Palladium
Venture if you dare
The legendary club of South London
Where venom fills the air

In loose control genial Malcolm Hardee
Takes shabby to a whole new level
But his unique style and exhibitionism
Ensure the crowd always revel

Expectation fills the room
As the seats all start to fill
Expectation the act will die
And 9 out of 10 times they will

So Malcolm takes to the stage
About to start the show
The 'open spot' acts wait there
Like prisoners on death row

Such an intimidating arena
They are far from a passive crowd
For if they aren't heckling for all they're worth
They are humming as one, very loud.

To be hummed off is disconcerting
But painful it's really not
Painful is when you're heckled off,
Followed by a flying pint pot.

But if you persevere with it
And some even make it through
It's a pretty good achievement
And a bloody hard thing to do.

The whole experience is daunting
For every single act
And many a time the aim is just
To keep dignity intact

So drink to the sadly departed
Both The Tunnel and Malcolm too
A huge part of comedy history
With recognition way overdue.

Young love

It'd be real grand,
If you'd hold my hand,
As we're walking up to school.
My mates would laugh,
They'd think I'm daft,
But I'm not playing the fool.

They can call me names,
Play their silly games,
I don't care what they do.
Just to get one smile,
I would walk a mile,
Because I'm in love with you.

I'd carry your books,
For one of your looks,
I'd do anything that you say.
I'd make myself smart,
I'd give you my heart,
I'd share my Milky Way.

So will you be mine,
Till the end of time,
And make this feel like heaven.
Cos I'll love you,
For forever too,
Or at least until year seven.

It's time to think again

When your lust no longer sparks the flame
When you've got nobody else to blame
When the memory man forgets his name
When your new songs all sound the same
When Spiderman has arachnophobia
When the lift attendant's got claustrophobia
The Olympic swimmer's hydrophobia
The arsonist has pyrophobia
When the tears of a clown turn his smile to a frown
And it's no longer funny when he falls down
And the high wire act fears leaving the ground
When the sado-masochist hates to be bound
When you can't find your way to the lost and found
When the flasher waits till there's no one around
When the whole place seems like a real ghost town
When your balls hang down like a basset hound
When MI5 have no more spies
When the MPs have run out of lies
When the bakery's run out of pies
There's no Goon show or Morecambe & Wise
When the actor can't get any good parts
When the singer can't get into the charts
When the gigolo no longer breaks hearts
When you start classing pool and darts as the arts
When the comedians no longer make you laugh
When you dread the thought of a photograph

When the bird fancier loses his homing pigeon
When the priest is doubting his religion
When Jehovah's witnesses stop calling
When there's no one on twitter worth trolling
When the naturist keeps on his jacket
When Bear Grylls can no longer hack it
When the circus juggler keeps dropping his clubs
When your team has used up all its subs
When the star centre forward couldn't see the goal
When the ageing golfer couldn't find the hole
When the weight lifter suffers from weakened wrists
When the champion boxer can't clench his fist
When the navigators got no sense of direction
When the porn star can't get an erection

It's time to think again

Wi-fi

My wi-fi runs out soon
My network's going to go
I'll no longer be able to chat
To those I hardly know
I'll have to face real people
And handle them alone
And hope they understand
I only whine and moan.
(I much prefer my phone)

I have no lifi
Without my wi-fi.

Hallowe'en

There are pumpkins in the window
Skeletons hanging down
There's Dracula and zombies
And a lairy scary clown
They're on the hunt for sweeties
Coming down your street
Knocking on your door
They ask you 'trick or treat'
You look into their little eyes
As up your path they roam
'No this isn't America
So go and piss off home'.

Santa

The kids were all excited,
Christmas party time was here,
But not all were so delighted,
Father Christmas was on the beer.

There was chaos and much confusion,
The whole point had been missed,
The mood had turned to disillusion,
The day Santa turned up pissed.

The alcohol had been flowing,
Santa was a merry fella,
The grotto was where he was going,
With a sackful of Cider and Stella.

He'd hands like a big red octopus,
Grabbing without any fear,
Causing more than a little fuss,
As he groped a stuffed reindeer.

Whether be an elf or a fairy,
All the lot of them got kissed,
Things were getting worryingly scary,
The day Santa turned up pissed.

He headed off for the buffet table,
With massive greed in his eyes,
But he was far from being able,
Threw up all over the pies.

The party ended abruptly,
No presents there to pick,
Just an overweight comatose Santa,
Collapsed and covered in sick.

So the children disappointed were leaving,
Still holding their presents list,
There were fewer kids now believing,
Since the day Santa turned up pissed.

Then struggling to his feet,
And grabbing one last beer,
Santa muttered 'well that was pretty neat'
'Same time again next year?'

Bob

Bob's a wheeler dealer he's an eye for a deal,
He'll buy anything he can get for a steal .
He wanders around picking up odds and sods,
Will never be caught paying over the odds.
He's always first in to get the best picks,
He's a wily old bugger who knows all the tricks.
He'll buy anything be it new or old,
Whether antiques or records, jewellery or gold.
He knows in his mind and he'll never deny it,
He's always got a punter lined up to buy it.
Might seem like he's just there for the craic,
But watch him, he'll have the shirt off your back.
Bob's a wheeler dealer, there's nothing he's not sold
And although he'll nail yer hat on, he's got a heart of gold

I've gotta stop drinking whisky

She was all alone at the Market Arms
Susceptible to all my charms
The price she charged then raised alarms
I've gotta stop drinking whisky

I slightly over ran my date
Upped my normal consumption rate
Arrived at work a good 4 hours late
I've gotta stop drinking whisky

Cracking night with Dave my chum
We downed the scotch with tots of rum
Ended up with a tattooed bum
I've gotta stop drinking whisky

Coming home at half past three
Walked face first into a tree
Ended up in A and E
I've gotta stop drinking whisky

Took a girlfriend to a party
Feeling lucky, hale and hearty
But I finished before I'd started,
I've gotta stop drinking whisky

I need to think about my health
Then stay away from that top shelf
I wake up and I've pissed myself
I've gotta stop drinking whisky

So no more whisky, there it's said
I'll safely sleep in a dry clean bed
I'll just have beer and wine instead
Now I've stopped drinking whisky

It's our Earth !

There's manmade disaster on a global scale
The world as we know it is starting to fail
The ice caps are melting at a worrying pace
It's a very real threat to the human race
The times we are in hold serious troubles
CO2 levels have almost doubled
The planet is heating up by degrees
Clean water in shortage results in disease
Communities damaged as temperatures rise
The impending demise should be no surprise
Rain forest rape desecrating a nation
Destroying habitats with deforestation
Plastic drastically drifts in the breeze
Polluting the poisoned and warming seas
Eight million tonnes in the oceans each year
I fear it's clear it won't just disappear
Industrial farming and over consumption
Non organic methods cause food chain disruption
Vast quantities of goods that are never tasted
As one third of all produced food is wasted
With greed for power and race hate wars
Famine and pain and homelessness caused
Insufficient crops to feed growing populations
Inequality between struggling nations
We have to act now to put the world right
It's not going to just all go right overnight
Use renewable energies to power the masses
Reduce fossil fuels to cut greenhouse gasses
It's my world it's your world it's all that we've got
Look after it now before this earth is shot.
Make haste in this race to erase this disgrace
Cut waste, cut waste, cut waste, don't waste !

Jim McDonald

Jim McDonald a psycho chap
Give you a smile then give you a slap
He'll be in The Rovers having a chill
So he will

He had twin sons who didn't look alike
A wife called Elizabeth who must have had a bike
He was wanted by the police and so he often hid
So he did

Had a distinctive Irish lilt
Was quite stocky and heavily built
Liz thought he was a thug, so she got rid
So she did

Jim McDonald almost every night
Would be out spoiling for a fight
He'd fight all day long if he could
So he would

His Corry character started to fail
So his story line was to put him in jail
And people now say Jim Mc who?
So they do

Doggin

Went for a walk late last night
Got myself a moonlight fright
Couldn't quite believe the sight
Surely all this can't be right
Doggin

Exhibitionist delight
Having sex by dimmed flashlight
Everything is quite forthright
Sweaty bodies packed in tight
Doggin

An abundance of skin
There's fat and there's thin
It's time to begin
On the car park of sin
Doggin

You just park up your car,
It may seem quite bizarre,
Be Mini or Jaguar,
Your own mobile boudoir.
Doggin

They're all at it there
In acts of despair
They don't seem to care
Bums and legs in the air
Doggin

The windows are steaming
Performing full beaming
There's moaning and screaming
And internet streaming
Doggin

It's a sport for spectators
For sexual creators
It's for all deviators
You can watch fornicators
Doggin

So if you want to star
And you feel up to par
In full view in your car
A true dogger you are

Doggin - Car park clogging
Doggin - Windscreen fogging
Doggin - Limelight hogging
Doggin - There's not much snoggin
Doggin - Sure beats jogging.
Doggin - We all love doggin !

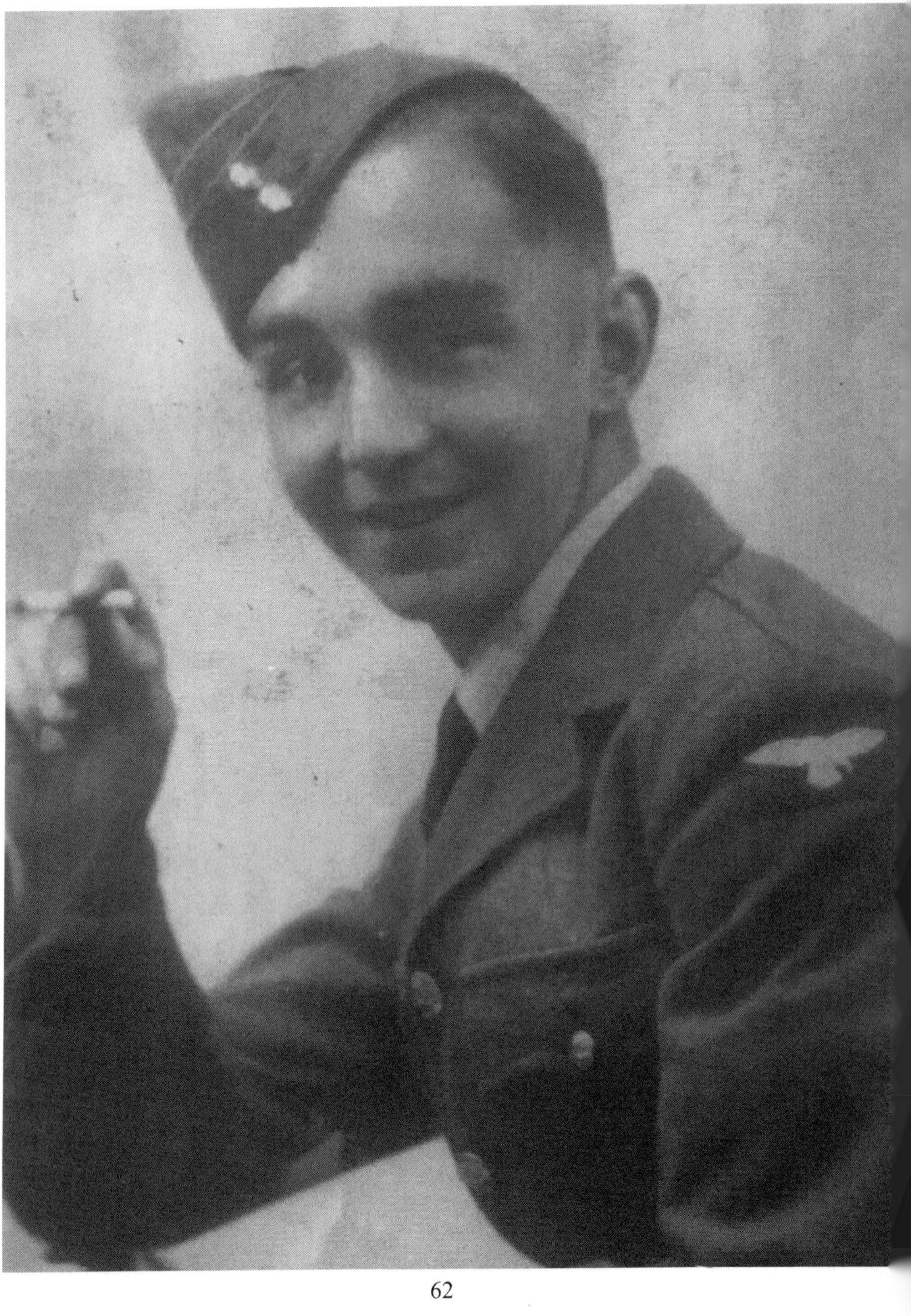

Jack

What would I do today
If my dad was here
Might take him out for dinner
Might take him for a beer
Might catch up on all things,
Have a good long chat
And tell him that I love him,
Long time since I did that
I'd take him into town
That would be a nice surprise
And show him all the places
That he'll hardly recognise
Stroll around the cricket field
That was his pride and joy
Where I would watch him play
Every weekend as a boy
And reminisce about the times
And all the passing years
And we would have a lot of laughs
And maybe shed a tear
But all that could never happen
So this is all I'll say
Keep fresh all those memories
Everyday's my Father's Day

Happy 'whatevers' Day

Father's Day
Mother's Day
Any bloody others day.
Just a game
Just a trend
Another way to make you spend.
Make an effort
Make a show
Once a year to let them know.
Make them wanted
Make it real
Take them for some shitty meal.
Buy them flowers
Buy them chocs
Like birthdays but without new socks.
It's not from you
It's a farce
Just for once get off your arse.
Life is good
When you share
In that moment show you care.
But it's commercial
It's enforced
It's what's expected now of course.

So happy Easter /
Halloween
Or anytime we reconvene.
So thanks for life
And thanks for health
And thanks for thinking for yourself.
To show your love
Before you're old
When you feel, not when you're told !

Happy 'Clintons' payday.

Poetry

They ask me what poetry is
It's a way of communication
It's a method, a mode, a message
And maybe alliteration
A thought, an idea, proposition
Suggestion of how something goes
A plan to scan attention span
Manifesto set out in prose
The writing of thoughts can be
Cathartic and revelatory
Give help to cope and hope
Be new and anticipatory.
Take chances and speak how you feel
Progression from here to create
In your mind what you wish to reveal
Spell it out and articulate
So say what is poetry then
It's really nothing confusing
It's the thoughts that flow from the pen
In the order of your choosing.

Let's

Let's get drunk it's been a while
Acting like some juveniles
We will hit the town in style
Taking it the extra mile

Let's book a room somewhere cheap
Let's talk about matters deep
Let's go to bed but not to sleep
Let's make promises we won't keep

Let's plan for a future we won't see
In our Utopia you and me
Make love all night and then agree
It's time that we were both set free

Let's pretend that we're not lovers
Take no notice of the others
Know that we won't be discovered
Live our lies beneath the covers

We'll say we set the world alight
Away from all that's crass and trite
But soon enough we'll just take flight
And steal away into the night

Dog walk, by the sea (for Sharon)

See the dogs run round cheery
While I stand there weary
It's the price that you pay for your pets
In all types of weather
You're out there together
But it's your choice there are no regrets

Feel the winds, the gusts
The powerful thrusts
That blast over the beach from the seas
I'm looking forlorn
In a crazy sandstorm
As I shelter a while from this breeze

Now my face is frozen
With ice from the ocean
The salt water's stinging like mad
I just feel downtrodden
My clothes are all sodden
It's all just got a bit bad

And the waves are churning
And no one's learning
As they thrash the wall with their might
And the spray to the sky
Must go twenty feet high
Showering all in its sight

So heading back home
With 'poor me' syndrome
Dogs, fed and watered, now tired
Take a large glass of wine
The world will be fine
As you curl up in front of the fire

Across the bay

Gazing across the vast bay,
Sun down at the close of day,
And the two of us flirted,
On a beach deserted,
As the tide just ebbs away.

And the feeling of peace is there,
And there's stirrings of love in the air,
Whatever we do,
It's just me and you,
For the rest I really don't care.

And the mountains that rise o'er the sea,
In the distance majestically,
Stand bold and tall,
Looking down on us all,
And are solid as are you and me.

Love poem 2

You're as easy to predict as the lottery
You're as clear as a Beckett play
You're as shallow as a snakes foot spa
You're as warm as an Arctic day

You're as calming as a prison riot
You're as cuddly as a rabid dog
You're as safe as a field of land mines
You're as subtle as a marshland bog

You're as chatty as Marcel Marceau
You can bore and bore all day
You're not the easiest to get to know
You've fuck all of interest to say

You're as straight as the Tower of Pisa
As delicate as a roaring Harley
You're as smooth as a bike on cobbles
As welcoming as Checkpoint Charlie

You're unwanted everywhere you go
As tempting as a cold Greggs pasty
Your mood swings like a pendulum
You've a predominance for turning nasty

Your empty dead eyed stare
Like the shark before the kill
You avoid me all you can
Like you used to do, the bill

You're nothing but a user
Nothing but a teaser
Your heart couldn't be colder
If you kept it in a freezer

So why don't you carry on turning
You don't seem to have a care
Walk in the direction of oblivion
You'll be in your element there

You're the epicentre of my misery
You're a dart in the heart of my pain
You're the legendary bad penny
Please, please don't turn up again.

Mum

I imagine the first word I uttered was mum
In between crying and sucking my thumb
And I've carried on saying it every day
As you've always been there in every way
And I wonder if I ever really said 'ta'
For being my mum and the woman you are
And the time that you spent on putting us first
Always there at the times, the best and the worst
Unerringly selfless always a hand
To spare, to share, to make everything grand
And you worked and worked as much as able
To look after us all, to put food on the table
And cook and clean and send us off neat and tidy
And treat us to a Chippy tea on a Friday
We always came first, that seemed your priority
And you brought up our family with loving authority
Every cut every graze attended by mum
And in those days of recklessness there sure were some
I don't know how you coped, three men in the home
We were messy, untidy would grumble and moan
But you had our measure you had us sussed
And you always came good and never a fuss
I couldn't imagine how life would have been
Without you, we love you, Mum.....Gran.... Jean.

XX

Life goes on

They say - from a good place
'If there's anything I can do.....'
And you say I'm ok thanks
But what you mean to do

Is say

Text me
Phone me
Don't stay away
It's ok
Face time
Face to face time
Anytime
Call and see
I'm still me
Drop in for coffee
Call for tea
Hug me
Invite me out
Don't leave me out
Keep me in the loop
Keep me in the group
Tell me the news
Keep me amused
Don't edit conversation

Talk openly
It's fine
Talk of the past
Yours and mine
Talk of the future
Don't treat me differently
Nothing's broke
Feel free to joke
Don't walk on eggshells
You won't offend me
We can still have fun
Life goes on

Road rage

Road rage road rage
Have a go at any age
Ranting raving
Highway misbehaving
Daring not caring
Shouting and swearing
Argue the principle
Think you're invincible

Road rage road rage
Vintage or teenage
Heavyweight or frail old girl
Think you can take on the world
Carving up blasting horn
Braking hard just to warn
Don't do this don't do that
Don't linger there don't be a twat

Road rage road rage
Trying to upstage
Wanna come wanna pass
Tailgating up my ass
Not so close back a bit
Stop behaving like a tit
Shout out giving it
Don't take any shit

Road rage road rage
Even in old age
Face off wrinkly faces
Zimmers at 20 paces
Road rage road rage
Acting your mental age
Ain't scared of no one
Not afraid to throw one
Road rage road rage
Looking like a stone age
Like a monkey in a cage
Everlasting road rage.

X Factor

I feel a pain down to the bone
Switch off TV, leave me alone
The X factor makes me want to groan
I've got Irritable Cowell Syndrome !

Summertime fades

As summertime began to fade
And spring had long ago gone by
The final act had just been played
An emptiness behind the eye

And he felt the feelings coming on
From the stark the dark was calling
Feeling week and so withdrawn
All he heard was hail falling

And he saw things through a shimmering light
No focus any direction he ran
And didn't know how to win this fight
There never was a master plan

A chance just on a mood pursued
A stance a need a plea to aid
No attitude for gratitude
Abandoned left alone afraid.

I'm always here

Remember that I'm always here
Whenever you may need me
A friendly hand to hold on to
And chat whenever need be

Someone to share your thoughts
Each and every day.
To talk of any worries
And take them all away.

And if you go through dark times
I'll be there to shine a light.
I'll hold you through the daytimes
And hug you through the night.

I'll reassure you through uncertainty
How ever hard it seems.
And drive away unpleasant thoughts
And take away bad dreams

Whatever goes I'm by your side
Just where I'll always be.
So please don't doubt for a minute that
The one for you is me.

Cobbled

The hobbled feet
On a cobbled street
He's chilled down to the bone
As they walk by
He'll get the eye
Vulnerable and alone

An open target
At a closed up market
A down and out, a fool
A hope of sobriety
Cast out from society
A figure of ridicule

Soaked wet through
And still they do
Contemptuous of his look
There for the picking
He'll get a kicking
They just don't give a fuck

Amongst the trash
A cut a gash
A bed of needles lie
But no correction
Just infection
Leaves him there to die

So one less crying
One less trying
One less pair of feet
Another sadistic
Enforced statistic
More blood on that cobbled street

Table for one

A place in the wrong time
Circumstance or fate
Subject of condition
That once called a date

Whispered and unanswered
Unheard in a void
Response is an echo
Relations destroyed

Alone in partnership
Rhetorical conversation
Imagined company
Inevitable destination

No social calendar
There's limited fun
Left only with thoughts now
A table for one

Punk – an attitude

It was Seventy Six
And our feelings were mixed
And confusion, disillusion
Were things to be fixed
But we found in a sound
And they said it was punk
We were hated and slated
They said it was sunk
Was it really so shocking
That blocking and barring
Marring progression
Of natural succession
But we rose and we chose
Individually grew
With a feeling believing
An attitude through
For this was the new
Pistols, Clash,
Buzzcocks
Dismiss trash
What for us rocks
Right out there
Clothes and hair
Westwood's passion for fashion
No one to tag on –
To any bandwagon

The word was heard
And shouted loud and proud
And how we blame the same
The bland that banned
Or tried to hand
A mark on us
And blame because
Of Teenage revolution
The seventies solution
The disco dissolution
Of mind numbing classroom pollution.
And we finally had a way of our own
A dawning day to own
And doors were opened
And class was crass
The system of society fragmented
Opinions vented
Bully power dissented.
So I say the day
That the attitude called punk
Was born of tired
Platitudes that stunk
Of hypocrisy
When after all in its day
Wasn't this in its way,
Just another replay
Of Presley, Little Richard
Who rocked and shocked
Of the putative 'Fab Four'

Who were all adored
Yet tore
The establishment to bits,
Well, if the cap fits
Change is nothing strange
 It's the excitement and rage
And coming of age
So face the race
And chase the empty space
Of the stagnant the redundant place
The festering face
Of banality to its finality
We went to satisfy our own end,
To buck the trend
And the choices of using our voices
For the truth that is youth.

So have it any way
Punk is an attitude
As relevant today

Will you be my valentine?

Will you be my valentine
Will you take a chance
Will you come with me today
Where we can find romance

And if you are my valentine
I'll treat you as the best
And maybe you'll be faithful
Unlike all the rest

Will you be my valentine
Will you be my lover
Will I be your only
Or will you shag another

Will you be my valentine
Will you be my spouse
Or will you soon grow tired of me
And piss off with my house

What you see is what you regret

What you see is what you regret
The memories were different though I'll bet
What you see in the bedroom after you're fifty
It may not be slim it may not be nifty
May be too much flab and too little flair
But you can bet the determinations still there
Don't give up hope just because
You may no longer look like Kate Moss
I may no longer look like one of Bros
Come to think of it neither of us ever was

The theory you can keep your youth is just a myth
You had a full length mirror now you have full width
And between sensual whispering voices
May be unintentional bodily noises
Don't go for that sexual hustle and bustle
You'll likely get cramp or pull a muscle
You were once a brave now you are big chief
Your underwear may not be quite as brief
Your drinking water glass now contains your teeth
The amount of pills you take beggars belief
Don't jump out of bed or you'll come to grief
You won't need an alarm so that's a relief
A glimpse of you naked will scare any thief

What you see is what you regret
Get yourself on the internet
Grab the handset and press reset
Your body's heavily in debt

What you see is what you regret
You're in a muddled middle age mind set
You live your life in a hot and cold sweat
Don't forget, don't fret, not finished yet

What you see is what you regret
This is what you get, life's a threat
Skip the sex just have the cigarette
You're no Romeo and Juliet

What you see is what you regret
What you see is what you
R.
E.
G.
R.
E.
T.
Regret

I turn to Jack

It's my life
That's for sure
I know I've faults
But I endure
I keep on going
I don't turn back
Cos when all else fails
 I turn to jack

I can turn to jack
And everything's good
The world looks the way
That I hoped it would
And the problems are clearer
There's nothing I lack
And if I find that there is
 I turn to jack

I turn to jack
For the courage I need
For the answers I seek
Satisfaction guaranteed
For the peace of mind
When I hit the sack
And if I can't sleep
 I turn to jack

I turn to jack
When the creditors come calling
When the days are dark
And I feel like I'm falling
When I think I should quickly
Slip out of the back
And give them some space
 I turn to jack

I turn to jack
Cos jacks always there
Unlike fair weather friends
Who don't really care
When I ask them for help
They are taken aback
But who gives a toss
 I turn to jack

I turn to jack
When I pick up the post
And burn all the bills
While making some toast
Or I would if there was
Any bread in the pack
But there's not, but no problem
 I turn to jack

I turn to jack
Time after time
Some can't see
Any reason or rhyme
But walk in my shoes
And avoid all the cracks
And see if you don't
Turn to jack

I turn to jack
So leave me alone
Just the two of us now
Belong in this home
You can stick around
If you want the craic
Or just forget it
I turn to jack

I turn to jack
And I get through the night
I wake in the morning
Feeling contrite
There's only regret
Nothing else there
More to forget
A trip to nowhere
So I turn back to jack
Puzzled and scared
There wasn't an answer
Seems nobody cared
The whole thing was just
My whole life soundtrack
That finally ended
When I turned to jack

I've never slept with Kate Moss

I've never run through wheat fields
Like the reckless Mrs. May
Neither left my country
In a state of disarray

I never went to Uni
I wasn't quite that big
Never went to Eton
Or been intimate with a pig

I've never been to Grimsby
Why go somewhere that starts with grim
As for going to Cockermouth
The chances are slim
(.........never going to Scunthorpe!)

I've never ordered quinoa
Or hummus or other dips
I'd rather play it safe
With good old fish and chips

I've never had a jäger bomb
Nor ever drunk a shot
I've never taken class A drugs
And hardly any pot

I've never eaten tripe or cowhell,
Offal or sheep's eyes
Having said that it's possible
As I've had Holland's meat pies

I've never seen the skyline of Manhattan
From The Hudson after dark
Never walked through the snow
At Christmas in Central Park

I've never thought to climb a mountain
Just because it's there
Or jump out of an airplane
And plummet through the air

I've never been to a Turkish barber
Where they all come out the same
Where a serious number one cut
Is the name of the barbers game

I've never been to the USA
I've never called women chicks
I've never sat on a Harley D
Or driven Route 66

I've never seen springtime in Paris
Or been up the Eiffel Tower
Just the one in Blackpool
Under a heavy shower

I've never done a bungee jump
Or been to Switzerland skiing
I've never seen the point I guess
I'm a boring human being

I've never driven a fast car
Around a racing track
I've never been to Ireland
And revelled in the craic

I've never snacked on caviar
Or sipped champagne from a flute
But I have on one occasion
Drunk Asti from a boot

I've never seen The Godfather
Casablanca or Citizen Kane
But I've seen Debbie does Dallas
Time and time again

I've never heard a country song
That had a happy ending
I've never been to a posh dinner dance
I feel I wouldn't blend in

I've never dined out
On an expense account lunch
I've never met a UKIP
I didn't want to punch

I've never danced in moonlight
Under sexy skies in Greece
But I have had a romp on Southport beach
And got sand in every crease

I'm not in the mile high club
It's just never come about
But there are lots more flights to do
So I've not yet ruled it out

So I'm going to make a great big list
Of all the things I'd like to do
And right at the top would be Kate Moss
And close second would be you.

Give me your worries

Give me your worries
Give me your fears
I'll take them away
I'll dry out your tears

Give me your problems
Give me your pain
I'll live them for you
Again and again

Give me your uncertainties
Reservations and doubts
Place them all in my care
And I will sort them out

For you can rely on me
To take away all the above
And all I ask in return
Is just, give me your love.

Coronation Street

There's a feeling of murder
And death in the air
There's a knowing that lives
Can be broken right there
There's a feel of mistrust
With the people you meet
It's just another day though
On Coronation Street.
There's divorce and affairs
And matters of the heart
Sex scandals abundant
As relationships part
On a northern street like this
You think anything will do
But there's gangsters, bigamists
And serial killers too
There are business manipulators
Embezzlers and cheats
It's all very clandestine
On this Weatherfield street

They get on with their lives
And nothing is hurried
But everyone knows
Where the bodies are buried
It's a land of danger
Where all seems quite bleak
And we all get to witness it
Five times a week !
But there are laughs too
As you see those feet
Hobble on the cobbles
Down Coronation Street

You are unique

We are all different
With a purpose to seek
What we are is original
Completely unique
We've individual aims
How our feelings are fired
And it's all there within
It's the way we are wired
This is all down to you
You've a reason to be
You've a life to live
A whole world to see
There are people to meet
Friends that you'll make
Battles you'll win
But also mistakes
It isn't all laughs
There are lows on the way
But more possibilities
Every new day
And that's what it's about
Taking your turn
Taking your chances
And that's how you learn
Feed the need not the greed
And embrace all you see

Make things happen
Let challenges be
Observe but don't judge
Look through and beyond
Reach and respect
React and respond
Environment, breeding
Background and class
These things will make you
When all are amassed
Look past the facade
And colour of skin
See with no prejudice
A place to begin
Advice will be offered
To take and to use
And you make the choices
To win or to lose
Tests and temptations
Are dropped at your door
Pressures and pitfalls
That mess you up more
So allow new thoughts
New feelings new cultures
And model your life
Like a beautiful sculpture
Shape your present
Map out your course

And head for the future
From a solid built source
As some will aim low
Some for the stars
Some will get lost
Between Venus and Mars
But you'll find your way
Via goals that you make
And seeing them through
At the moment you take
Look for the positive
Life has no sequel
Ignore the negative
Treat all as equal
While aiming for dreams
Don't look too high
Take opportunities
As they come by
Set your agenda
But keep a clear mind
Be open to opinions
And see what you find
Be true to yourself
Be honest, be strong
Don't be afraid
To admit that you're wrong
You set the standards
How your life should go

The thoughts and ideals
That only you know
So how things turn out
You can only sense it
You can't see the future
But you can influence it
So take all your plans
Your hopes and ideals
And work all you might
Till you feel they are real
Remember success
Isn't there on a plate
It's all down to your work
Don't leave it to fate.
Don't follow the crowd
Don't only make do
Live life your way
Let the crowd follow you.

Victoria

Victoria, the name of a talent outstanding
Focused perception and so self demanding
From her pen flows a torrent of magical words
From the lightest the brightest to purely absurd
Her humour and warmth, language and phrasing
Original and honest, nothing short of amazing
A stream of creation with no false pretences
That wake and explode and heighten the senses
A huge superstar on the stages she's pacing
Yet privately quiet and most self effacing
Uncanny depiction of any position
That quickly evokes a real recognition
So able to enlighten, surprise and disarm
With action and comedy, pathos and charm
The songs with the rhythm and perfect rhyming
The stories with well polished true comic timing
Her work is respected all over the nations
Meticulously crafted her comic creations
The acting, the writing, the sketches the songs
Took her to the top where she surely belongs
A trail of successes from big screen to small
'Stand up' and theatre, she just had it all
Loved by the millions that watch her TV
Who laugh loud and smile at all that they see
By all in the business the great and the good
It's that lass from Bury, Victoria Wood

Giving

I gave you a glance
You gave me a grin
I wanted to touch
Your silky smooth skin
I gave you my number
You passed me your card
I made a suggestion
You caught me off guard
I gave you a wink
You gave me a smile
I gave you an inch
You wanted a mile
I gave you a kiss
You turned on my light
I gave you my body
You gave me all night
I gave you affection
You held me real close
I gave you devotion
You gave me a dose !

Pick up yer dog shit

You can't choose where you walk these days
With hazards everywhere
The pavement is a mine field
And no one seems to care
There's a problem I've encountered
Taking the route I often use
It's a never ending nightmare
Getting dog muck on my shoes

And leaving mess is not an option
That I will allow
Pick up yer dog shit you dirty sod
Pick up yer dog shit
Now

I find it on the footpath
I find it on the road
I find the exact place
Where your dog dropped its load
So something needs to be done
And I just don't care how
Pick up yer dog shit you dirty get
Pick up yer dog shit
Now

Some people do a half job
And that incenses me
They put the turd in a little black bag
And hang it from a tree
Like a Christmas decoration
A poo bauble on the bough
Pick up yer dog shit you dirty bugger
Pick up yer dog shit
Now

Even at the beach now
Seems the way it goes
Slimy stinking dog cack
Oozing through my toes
If this filthy way continues
There's going to be a row
Pick up yer dog shit you dirty bugger
Pick up yer dog shit
Now

I seem to find the location
Whenever I'm about
And put my foot in the filthy place
That the dogs just curled one out
If I stand in dog shit one more time
There'll be trouble I will vow
Pick up yer dog shit you dirty bugger
Pick up yer dog shit
Now !

There's only so much I can take
And I won't tell you again
Pick up yer dog shit
PICK UP YER DOG SHIT !
And put it in a bin

End of the pier

Watch the sun go down at the end of the pier
Feel the mood as I'm sitting here
While the seagulls hover with elegant flair
A melancholia fills the air
You look and think and maybe reflect
And hope and wish don't just expect
Alone with your thoughts time to spend
And wonder will things ever mend
The dark the deep the mystifying
If there are rules there's no complying.
Sitting thinking much confusion
Looking for the right conclusion
The suns gone down at the end of day
And the fear on the pier will all go away
As a new day begins so what will you find
You can leave all bad thoughts and troubles behind
And pick up your bag lift up your feet
Move on along and retreat from defeat
Like that seagull that hovered and bided its time
And the angler who sits with his bait on the line
It's just about waiting planning and thinking
And then treading water to stop you from sinking

Fast Food

Fast food crass food
When you can't be assed food
End of the night food
After a fight food

Can't beat a bit of greasy fried chicken
Finger licking and makin sickin
Clogging up get the arteries sticking
Gonna make the struggling heart stop tickin

After the pub a Donna kebab
Essential food to feed the flab
Mix it up try to embellish
With chilli and mayo and buckets of relish.

Fast food crass food
When you can't be assed food
End of the night food
After a fight food

Deep pan pizza dripping with grease
Getting your fill while getting obese
Get it all on don't be fickle
Extra chips and extra pickle

Bring me some burgers every day
Eat them at work and eat them at play
Eat them regardless of how you look
Eat them until they make you puke

Fast food crass food
When you can't be assed food
End of the night food
After a fight food

Two poems dedicated to two of my poetry heroes
1. Hovis Presley - a tribute

I relied on you....
Cos a poet needs a hero
Like a fiddle needs a Nero
Like the 60s needed Helen Shapiro
Like a gangster film needs Robert DeNiro

I'll remember you ....
Like rainy holidays in Wales
When I'm drinking real ale
When I'm at a car boot sale
When I think of all your tales

I'll thank you...
For saying what you say
For showing me the way
For inspiring every day
For mastering downplay

I'm sad that you...
Aren't staying till full time
Are bowing out in your prime
Have no more poems sublime
Have a name that's hard to rhyme.

And Hovis too
We all miss you.

2. John Cooper Clarke

It was way back in the seventies
When I started writing poems
I didn't have any agenda
Didn't know where I was going

Poetry wasn't cool when I was at school
So I kept it in the dark
Till I came across this maverick guy
Poetically named John Cooper Clarke

He had a look of Bob Dylan
And words at least as strong
He wrote of things that mattered to him
Whatever right or wrong
He had a pretty unique style
Charismatic cool and dry
With a swipe at modern society
And a wink in his shaded eye
He was centre stage the rage of an age
The voice of a generation
A breath of fresh air of poetic flair
Of veritable veneration
He played with all the punk bands
Right in the thick of it
And coped and hoped and often groped
Through missiles and showers of spit

He spoke of his native Salford
With passion and power and pride
He never papered over the cracks
He'd nothing at all to hide
His image you'd spot a mile off
His sartorial elegance there
With pencil thin drainpipe trousers
And a mass of thick black hair
The trademark shades a giveaway
And that nasal Salford drawl
But when it came to the art of poetry
Johnny Clarke just had it all.
There have been many pretenders
But he set the real benchmark
The one and only the bard of Salford
Dr John Cooper Clarke

JCC signing his book of poems for me !

Mi Señora Española (My Spanish Lady)

There's a place that I know
Where my mind will often go
To a time,
Such a time,
A time I'll not forget

And I know in that place
I've a memory of a face
Now there's no trace
Of that face,
And I've nothing but regret

Your silken skin so smooth showered by your flowing hair
With elegance and style and a look beyond compare.
My Spanish lady

In that land of constant sun
Let my crazy feelings run
Going wild
Like a child
And my head was in a whirl

When we sat and we talked
Then we held hands and we walked
And I knew
As we grew
I would never lose that girl

Your silken skin so smooth showered by your flowing hair
With elegance and style and a look beyond compare.
My Spanish lady

Now it seems more like dreams
As I try to live those scenes
Things changed
Rearranged
Just down to circumstance

And I try not to cry
When I think I let it die
No love purer
Than my Señora
Yet it ends our one romance

Tu piel de seda tan suave bañada por tu cabello que fluye
Con elegancia y estilo y una belleza que no tiene comparación
Mi Señora Española.

Share

Let us share some wine
Let us share some time
Let me share your pillow tonight

Let me stare in your eyes
Let us share the sun rise
Let me stay and hold you tight.

Let me whisper so quiet
In my mind there's a riot
Never felt like this before

Let us keep it this way
For all of today
If not for evermore

Jellyfish

The sea's alive don't dare go in
No one today will have a swim
There's something lurking in the deep
Will hurt for fun will make you weep
I don't agree to kill for fun
But make exception with this one
The one thing in the world I'd wish
Is kill the bastard jellyfish
It's evil through and through that thing
With tentacles and nasty sting
Oh God had a sense of humour for sure
For the only way that you can cure
Is find just where the sting has hit
And have somebody piss on it
There's nothing redeeming about this thing
There's not a single pleasure to bring
You can't even cook it to make a dish
Of the nasty bastard jellyfish !

Goodbye to the Tyne, (for Tracey)

Goodbye to the Tyne
Got to go away
Love you for all time
Think about you every day

Like you I'll keep on moving
But my hearts in the same place
Transmuting and evolving
Never giving up the chase

Goodbye to the Tyne
And every bend and turn
You gave to me the sign
There's more out there to learn

Every twist you took
To the sea from source
I hold every part of you
In my heart of course

So goodbye to the Tyne
Got to go away
Forever will be mine
And I'll return some day

As I watch you thunder by
You fill my heart with fire
Your constant dogged flow
Does nothing but inspire

Good bye to the Tyne
It's here my thought remains
No worries I'll be fine
Like you're flowing through my veins

Goodbye to the Tyne.
I'll miss you and how
Goodbye to the Tyne
...............For now x

Doors

Doors that lead me to places I know
Portals to educate helping minds grow
Entrances through which the mind can now travel
Ways in to let all the secrets unravel

And through each door
A thirst for more
A chance to build
And to restore
To make as new
Like once before
Advances chances
To explore

Doors that open, and welcome and greet you
New people see, waiting there just to meet you
A challenge a life change, a reason to be
A door always open for you and for me

Hey Dorothy

Hey Dorothy

Don't follow the yellow brick road
You'll get bullshit by the load
There is no castle
You'll just get hassle
Just do what you are told

Hey Dorothy

Don't trust one that flies from the east,
Nor one that flies from the west,
They are low life dealers
Brain cell stealers
Just putting you to the test

Hey Dorothy

The weirdo's are all taking hits
They'll just have you in bits
Tin man's got no heart
The Lion's a tart
And the scarecrow is off his tits

Hey Dorothy
Don't patronise the little wise guys
Despite their size won't sympathise
Ignore their prancing
And laughable dancing
They're just Krankies in disguise

Hey Dorothy
All these crazy characters you find
That aren't very well defined
Do you ever feel
That they're not that real
It's all in your muddled fuddled mind.

Hey Dorothy
Come back from your fantasy time
Can't you see the obvious sign
You call it Oz
But we know the cause
You are really up on cloud nine

Hey Dorothy
I've advice so you'll shed this dread
We can help you to sort out your head
Have a nice cup of tea
Instead of dropping another 'E'
Before you trip off to bed.

    'There's no place like rehab'

Awareness

I don't doubt
When a light goes out
When they say 'snap out'
'Get a grip'
They quip
They mean well
But can't tell
This hell
This feeling
That isn't revealing
But inwardly testing
Not manifesting
Nothing's clear
Round here
Be sincere
Force a smile
For a while
Don't complain
Just retain
Within yourself
Your state of health
Don't let it out
Or talk about
Because we don't
We won't
I never have spoken
Or broken
My solitude
Through hurt accrued

This heartache
We partake
Alone at home
And the very fact
That the act
Of keeping it in
Of holding within
Is where it begins
It isn't only
Being lonely
Being bored
Feeling ignored
Where a full room
Is like a vacuum
With no purpose
In life
Where uselessness
Is rife
Isolation
Stagnation
Deflation
Are what you find
And how unkind
To the mind
Is seeing
Reality fleeing
And the sense of being
A lost face
A lost race
A cost faced

From a dark place
A stark place
A hopeless case
To taste the waste
Not just that
But a flat emptiness
A hole, not a whole
A hole in the soul
A void you can't avoid
A failing where flailing
Is violent
Where a shout is silent
You don't think
How far you can sink
Where fears
Fall on deaf ears
And peers
Think 'cheers' with beers!
Will solve all
Dissolve all
Problems
And it may
Today
For now
But how
Can I borrow
The courage for tomorrow
Or just hope
That I'll cope
Will I cope?

Click bait

Switch on the screen every time
First thing that you see
Enticements for what you need
For who you want to be

There's click bait everywhere you look
Got to have a press
The garbage it throws out at you
To hit you with more stress

It's adverts, adverts all the time
They'll all constantly try
To indoctrinate you to their ways
The message here is buy

Click here and see how the film star looks
At age eighty eight
Click here and learn to earn a grand
Without getting off your seat

Click here and improve your life
Be quick the clock is ticking
Click to find an amazing diet
Make sure you keep on clicking

They reel you in like helpless fish
You're just a number now
A statistic on their clickometer
A way to sell and how

So however tempting it looks
How to look twenty years younger
Search only when you need to do
Don't feed the clickbait hunger.

Dating profile

Ageing sex symbol
Well past his best
Spends most days sitting
In pants and a vest
Looking for partner
To share what's left
Desperately seeking something
As pretty bereft
Got all his own teeth
Own car and own joint
Never too worried
To disappoint
Standards essential
As long as they're low
There's nowhere at all
That he wouldn't go
So hurry along now
And grab for this pleasure
There'll be plenty of time
To regret at your leisure
So grow old together
For better or worse
And bring all your valuables
Bank book and purse.

High tide

The ruthless crashing waves are breaking
A thousand photos for the taking
Stroll through clouds of salty mist
Embrace the taste of nature's kiss
As winter tides thrash unforgiving
Churning with a lust for living
The ocean with its power on course
Relentless in its strength and force
Irrepressible rage is ever present
Ferocious, formidable, incessant.
To stand and watch to stop and stare
Will calmly drench the unaware
Scaring daring passing by
The chance to glance when tide is high
Dark and deep, fraught with danger
The wondrous spectacle of nature

The Hitman

A fighter, a legend, a hero to most
A model to boxing, this one man, the toast
Stands firm in the ring where no one could hide
As everyone cheers for 'The pride of all Hyde'
And the feeling was there with the fans all on side
A tight knit community that none could divide
Taking and making one fight at a time
It's all real no faking, just boxing sublime
In or out of the ring with courage to find
The power to act, the great strength of mind
As temptations lay bare, challenges cast
A need and a will conditioned to last
Facing the demons like any opponent
Gripping the day and embracing the moment
British light-welterweight, people's one choice
'Ricky the Hitman' they chant in one voice
From basic beginnings in lowly Moss Side
To the 'Heartbreak Hotel' for the real Mr Hyde
This Manchester star jokes of breakfasts and chips
With an endless stream of hilarious quips
A true gritty character who no one dictates to
A true City fan who like minded relate to
They challenge from far, they challenge from near
But their challenge is futile, the outcome is clear
If small in stature, in talent a giant
Determined, focused, single minded, defiant
A genuine guy, what you see's what you get
Commands such affection, such love and respect
To all of his fans a hero will be
Ricky The Hitman - MBE

War

A hundred years since
The guns went silent
An end to hatred,
Fear and violence?

And what can we show
For those hundred years
More wars, more death
More pain, more tears

But it goes on still
No lessons learned
The state of war
Is a grave concern

The waste in battle
Of life's beginners
In wars all lose
There are no winners

The young sent to die
Again and again
By words from the world's
Few angry men.

Who dictate our fate
That's swiftly sealed
Feed their greed and intolerance
And racist ideals

And as long as we choose
To mark different as wrong
Without integration
No help to belong

There will still be divisions
And cracks in the wall
And peace won't come soon
It may not come at all

Is it really so hard
To live all as one
And embrace what is different
Till different has gone

Enrich your lives
Enhance your days
And take in and learn
New cultures and ways

Would it even work out
If we all were the same
Or is it just that we
Need someone to blame

If you're offered a hand
Don't deride or despair
We've more love than we use
So don't hide it, but share.

Stressing

As you travel through life
If you find you're stressing
Don't go to Southport
It's bloody depressing

I get emails

I get emails to tell me my teeth could be whiter
And dieting pills that would make me lighter
And emails to offer me a mini break in Spain
And 10 per cent off if I choose to go again
A voucher from Woucher a coupon from Groupon
A handy little stick you can grab doggy poop on
Household gadgets you never dreamed you'd need
Dating sites with satisfaction guaranteed
Irrelevant emails that come about nonetheless
Like a caring home where I can go to convalesce
Or cheap theatre tickets for the musical Chess
Or a trip across Europe on the Orient express
Or a recipe for soup made with kale and watercress
For all of these I couldn't care any less
I get an email from Apple to upgrade my phone
An unscrupulous offer of a payday loan
An appeal to find a cure for diphtheria
Or an offer from a nice wealthy prince in Nigeria
I get emails asking me to compare the market
And airport car deals about where to park it
Constant offers of Amazon Prime
What eBay's chosen for me this time
And emails that show me the latest fashions
And sexy clothes that will help my passions
And emails to help me get more thrills
By supplementing my diet with little blue pills
Bombarded with sexual offers for reflection
A collection and selection for correction of erections

I'll have to think hard before my memory fails
But how did we get by before we got emails?

Imagine   (for firefighters)

Imagine....
It's another day at work
And you're paid by the hour
And you walk through the doors
Into a blazing tower
It's just another day at work
On the edge of a knife
As every step you take
May be the one that ends your life
Just another day at work
Where lives are devastated
And the powers pass the buck
Self preservation motivated
Just another day at work
With job and minds inflamed
Where risking all each day
To then be handed blame
Just another day at work
A work where hell is seen
Where bureaucrats can't comprehend
And build their blameless screens
Another day at work
More horrors are endured
The sights and sounds unspoken
But competence assured
Another day at work
While family sit alone
And don't know day to day
Whether you'll return back home
Another day at work
........Imagine

Just for you

I love to hear a smidgen
Of cooing wood pigeon
The squawk of a hawk up above
And the harsh and graven
Call of the raven.
Or the beauty that's brought by the dove.

Hear the gentle rustle
Of the breeze through the trees
As slowly the first leaves are falling
And as you look down
The brown on the ground
A sign that Autumn is calling

As the low sun shines
Through the branches of the pines
And the gleam on the stream makes me dream
Of the sun that shone
Through the summer that's gone
On our faces in the places we've been.

Like the story of life
The seasons bring strife
Or would flood with good if they could
But each time of year
Brings cheer not just tears
To show how to grow as we should.

So look all around
And astound at the sound
And the sights and lights there to view
And try to remember
All year to December
It's all for the taking by you

Live to love

Love to live
Live to give
Give to share
Share to care
Care to show
Show to grow
Grow to be strong
Be strong to belong
Belong to be part
Be part of the heart
The heart of community
Community of unity
Unity together
Together whatever
Whatever will be
Will be to see
To see what is sought
Sought to be taught
Taught to achieve
Achieve to believe
Believe to do
Do to be true
Be true to survive
Survive to thrive
Thrive to succeed
Succeed to feed
Feed to relive
Relive to forgive
Forgive to live
Live to love

Look

Stand right up to me
Look straight at my face
Look into my eyes
To that darkened place
And what do you see
But oceans of grey
Horizons of pleasure
So, so far away
And you hurt and you cry
You're confused and shocked
And all of your options
Appear to be blocked
So push down the walls
Obstructing the way
Blow away the black clouds
Which gather each day
Unravel my thoughts
Untangle my mind
Sift through my feelings
See what you can find
Fight through the dark
Get into the core
Use your key to life
To unlock the door
And once you are in
The feeling is new
Embrace the clarity
Of light that's from you
You think your nightmare
May well never end
Share it with me
And you've got a friend

Looking at you

You look as though you're losing it
Your bits look like they've dropped
You should ask for your money back
If you've been to the body shop

You're not the person you once were
Your beauty's in the past
Your hair is in the plug hole
And your teeth are in a glass

Your figure isn't what it was
With the calories you consume
You're not so big on the dance floor now
Yet you do take up more room

You walk along the street now
Turning stomachs more than heads
Most of your friends are incontinent
The rest of them are half dead

And as I stare here at you
It almost makes me cry
As an old man stares back at me
The mirror doesn't lie !

Harvey Nix

Five hundred quid for a handbag !
One and a half grand for a coat !
Two hundred quid for a tea shirt !
It really doesn't float my boat.

The ladies who lunch of Manchester
In their cosy posy gear
Sip a five pound latte in the restaurant
Or an eight quid glass of beer.

In Harvey Nix they strut their stuff
Shopping the time away
Inflated price but they think it's nice
I can sit and watch all day.

I get my kicks
Watching pricks
On route
To Harvey Nix.

This is dedicated to the staff of the Christie hospital

To futures

To a fixed early date
On a rainy Manchester morning
To a labyrinth of angels
On a daily duty calling

To be ready
A must
To give all
To trust

To the dreaming room
To tenderness and care
To the expertise and skill
To the dedication there

To an end
To tears
To the future
Cheers

.

Clumsy

I wanted to be a goal keeper
But I couldn't hold on to the ball
I wanted to be a juggler
But I kept on dropping them all
I wanted to swing on flying trapeze
But I let my partners fall
Tried my hand at dry stoning
But made a pile of bricks from a wall

They say it's just because
I've no coordination in my head
If I go near a china shop
It fills them full of dread
There were none of these occupations
Where I could make some bread
So I decided I would become
A baggage handler instead

Snail in the garden.

Oh little snail
I see your trail
Chomping on my plants
Go eat some weeds
Not my lettuce leaves
Don't get me in a rant

You would find more
If you went next door
There's lots to choose from there
So leave my stuff
I've had enough
You're going to make me swear

I've asked you twice
And I've been nice
But this is what my pledge is
I sure will bet
That you'll regret
If you don't get off my veggies

So here is where I'm going
To keep the food chain flowing
And I'm no kind of nutter
But if I meet you
I will eat you
Dipped in garlic butter !

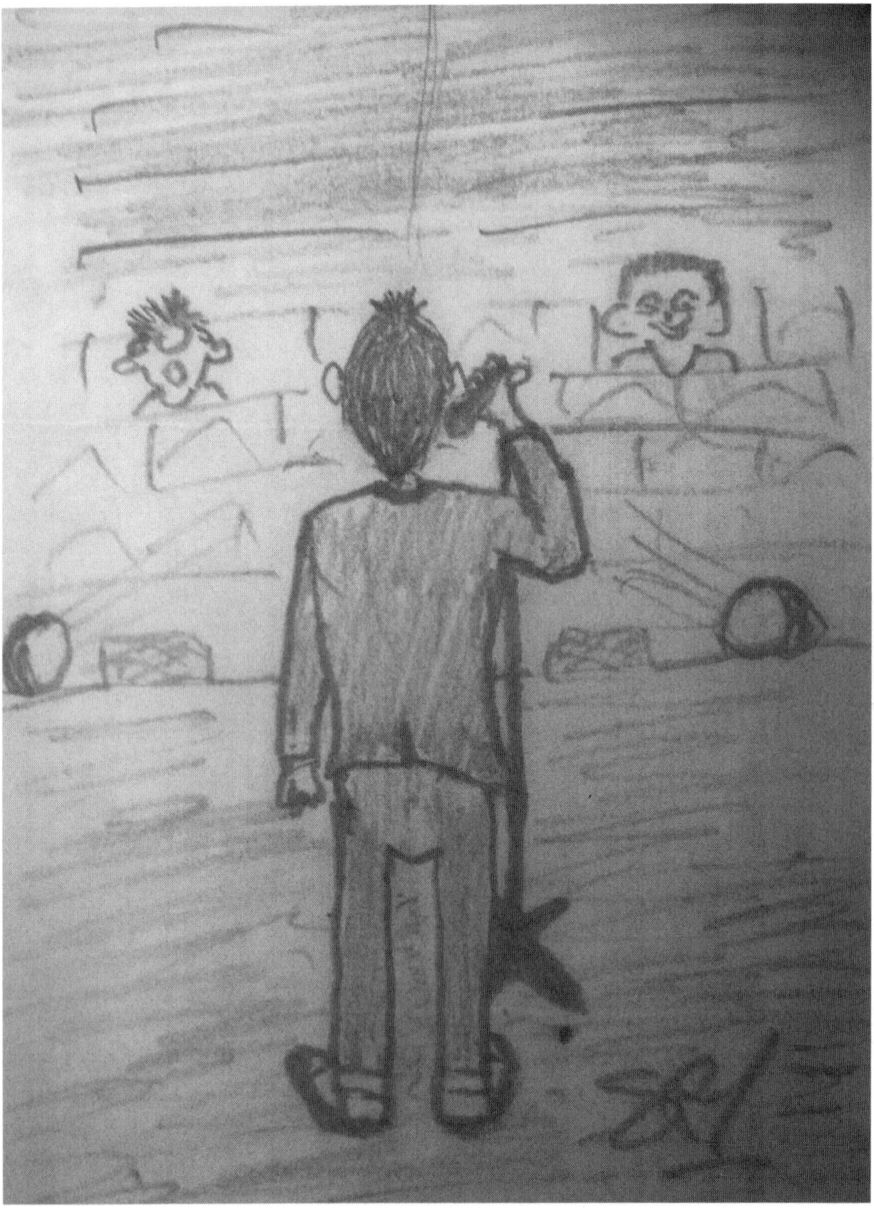

Show must go on

I played last night to a crowd of two
Not really sure what I should do
It's better than playing to a crowd of one
And as we know the show must go on
So I trundled through my structured set
I thought 'with luck I'll get them yet'
And persevered with my reciting
Hoping to be quite delighting
I started feeling pretty good
Was going the way I hoped it would
As I belted out a line sublime
They went to the toilet at the same bloody time !
I stood there staring at the wall
Talking to nobody at all
Not really sure of the protocol here
So I nipped to the bar for another beer
When they returned we closed the show
All was done and time to go
But not before I had some luck
And both the audience bought my book
To sell to everyone in the crowd
I really did feel rather proud
100 per cent is quite a sell
Not even 'Ed Sheeran' could do that well !

My lad

More than a loyal companion and friend
A unique friendship that could never end
A friend without agenda or any condition
Unlike most humans complete dedication
More than a dog much more than a pet
As much a part of the family you'll get
Who made my life far more worthwhile
Who conjured up a beaming smile
He'd make me happy when I was sad
Make me feel better when feeling bad
If I'm feeling low he'd cheer me up
With one lick from that loving pup
And what did he desire but caring
And to spend our time together sharing
And the greatest thing I think I learned
Was the un-ending love that was returned
Just to be given walks and lots of play
And share the best parts of the day
The simple joys we shared together
At any time in any weather
With no demands just love to give
Boundless energy, a life to live
Find a stream, a puddle, a lake
Straight in there make no mistake
But he will be straight back you bet
And shake till we're both soaking wet
He'll run and jump with balls and sticks
And I would teach him silly tricks

And that time when he ran away
I walked the streets and cried all day
Until he bounded back in sight
My tears turned back to pure delight
Forgiveness was an easy task
Always was, no need to ask

But when we were finally parted
And I was left there broken hearted
And the gap that's left in my life now
They say will ease I don't see how
For that the worst day of my life
When I had to say a last goodbye
You put those smiles upon my face
You made my world a better place
When I think of all we used to do
I will everyday miss and think of you
To the best friend that I'd ever had
Love and thanks, rest peacefully lad

The return

A greying landscape of tenement towers,
Plastic window boxes home to plastic flowers,
He runs between buildings dodging the showers,
Up from the south been driving for hours.

Back to his old home drove through the night,
Knowing full well there would be no delight,
And struck with this a heart breaking sight,
From where he had long since taken flight.

The place he'd grown, from where he came,
His hopes and dreams, the goals he'd aimed,
Nothing could ever stay the same,
Now all he felt was loss and shame.

Was it really wrong to aim for more,
To know ones mind to set ones store,
To knock at opportunities door,
So why the hell to feel so sore.

All he did was to take his chance,
To make a steady life advance,
If you don't ask you don't get that dance,
Or was it just a fairy tale romance.

So staring at the building through pouring rain,
A sight he'd seen time and time again,
Familiar yet this now caused him pain,
His happy nostalgia had been in vain.

His memories were of afar,
Deep down he could still feel the scar,
After all you really are who you are,
He turned and got back in his car.

Never ending smiles

Never ending smiles so sweet
The magic happens when we meet
If only it could be complete
.....Seeing you
Never ending smiles and glances
Never went and took the chances
Now I know how hard romance is
.....Wanting you
Never ending smiles and kisses
Dreams fulfilled with loving wishes
Now I know that only this is
.....Having you
Never ending smiles have gone
Memories now of lasting fun
Hoping that I'm still the one
.....Missing you
Never ending smiles that haunt me
Mixed emotions teasing taunt me
Wonder did you ever want me
.....Is it you
Never ending smiles in sight
Thinking of you day and night
Wishing I could hold you tight
.....Loving you
Never ending smiles I steal
And memories I can always feel
Maybe when the feelings real
.....I'll have you.

Scarlett (for Joanne and David)

There's a road
That we took
As a pair,
As we grew
As we love
As we care,
All the hopes
That we both
Used to share,
....When our hearts met.

What a life
That we wish
When we meet,
And a way
That we made
It complete,
As we wait
For the moment
We greet,
....Our little starlet.

And the love
That we shared
From the start,
Joins up now
With one new
Beating heart,
And our lives
Have a magic
New part,
.....And that's Scarlett

The Pub

For a community in unity
The pub is the hub
The centre of leisure
With its drink and it's grub
And the folk that make
The pubs great glories
With their tales and jokes
And real life stories
Who welcome new faces
To these communal places
Where all the world's problems
Are daily debated
And new friends are made
Affections displayed
And new partnerships
And relationships played
Entertainment is there
So let down your hair
Party at your local
Like you really don't care

It's a place to live
To enjoy life, to give
And together forever
Whoever you're with
Will join in the fun
The community run
The feeling of being
A part has begun
And the new friends you take
Real people not fake
It seems fine online
But here real friends you make
So though life's so busy
Relax with some quizzin
Love music- you choose it
Or dance yourself dizzy
So put down your phone
Don't sit there alone
Be vocal in your local
Let it be your new home.

Love is

Love is
Commitment, loyalty, caring
Love is
Dedication, giving, sharing

Love is
Infatuation, trust, obsession
Love is
Understanding, listening, compassion

Love is
Openness, candidness, clarity
Love is
Faith, hope, charity

Love is
Togetherness, oneness, unity
Love is
Sincerity, integrity, purity

Love is
Lust, passion, yearning
Love is
Devotion, desire, learning.

Love is
Contribution, risk, investment,
Love is
Judgement, appraisal, assessment

Love is
Intuition, instinct, sense
Love is
Emotion, insight, immense

Love is
Indication, focus, reflection
Love is
Consideration, thought, affection

Love has more ingredients than in any meal
Love is the most satisfying any one could feel
Love is a mystery there for the solving
Love is an unknown ever evolving
Love is depending on who you are with
Love could be all, but could be a myth
Love is a thought of what could be
Love is expensive, love is free
Love is not wanting to be apart
Love is one in two beating hearts
Love is a feeling down deep inside
Love manifests in a way one can't hide
Love is demeanour producing a mood
Love feeds life as surely as food
Love is confusing, whoever designed it
Love is the best, I hope that you find it

Reboot

Regardless of random reactionary rebels
Resurgence remains reassured
Rightwing revolutions rendered redundant
Rationality and reasoning restored

Normandy remembered

Sixth of June
Nineteen forty four
At Normandy, troops
Advanced on the shore
In numbers unheard of
By air and by sea
Sheer determination
For you and for me
So hard to imagine
The selfless deeds
For King and country
For all our needs
A will so strong
To take the task
Devotion, loyalty
No questions asked
As they hit the land
They opened the doors
Paved the way with
Troops flooding the shores
Still as you look back
Can't dry up the tears
Nor ever comprehend
The blind faith, the fears

And there see the outcome
Yet what of the cost
Count every one life
Twenty two thousand lost
Somebody's father
Somebody's son
The price in lives
Is that what was won?
Through patriotism
Boys only just men
Knowing they may not
See their families again
And they gave their all
To never cease
So we could all live
With freedom in peace

Home Gardens

There's something in the air in Home Gardens
It's something that people avoid
A place you and me, don't want to be
Where compassion is almost devoid
There are benches covered in papers
That point to the occupant's plight
And a horrible stench of urine
That lingers from Saturday night
There's a little old lady sitting
Feeding the birds as she does
And a down trodden guy in hi-vis
Scooping dog muck with no fuss
There's a gang of youths stood together
Just spitting on the ground
And swearing in their loudest voices
For the pleasure of all around
There's a dodgy looking bloke in black
Trading from his inside pocket stall
Little white packages of something
Distributing to one and to all
There's something in the air in Home Gardens
Where the pigeons outnumber the rest
With those that are scraping a living
A living of life past it's best

The lonely man goes through the bins
He's lost and bereft of a friend
Just searching for a half eaten pasty
Or a few potential fag ends
There's a woman at the side of the road
Her life is a full time recession
Sitting with a couple of plastic bags
Containing her whole lives possessions
It's a side of life that's often hidden
A world of misfortune and lies
A dark place that we don't recognise
As we avert our minds and eyes
A man slept in Home Gardens last night
His meaning not justified
And he lay deathly still this morning
With his last needle down by his side
Yes there's something in the air in Home Gardens
Showing serious social stagnation
There's need and greed and various misdeeds
And that air ..... is of desperation !

Piccadilly Lily

Piccadilly lily
Piccadilly lily
She drives men silly
Round the streets of Piccadilly

She offers favours
She calls them dates
She's special rates
For certain mates

Her past was bleak
Her future's stark
But she gives good service
Round the back of Primark

From early January
To the end of December
She's always on call
For a quick knee trembler

She works in the sunshine
She works in the rain
She always says thank you
Please come again

Piccadilly lily
Piccadilly lily
She drives men silly
Round the streets of Piccadilly

She has a little menu
Where everything's priced
With special discount
If you manage it twice

Just read through the options
Find your fave and pick it
Or to get the best value
You can book a season ticket

She makes things rise
She makes things hard
And when she leaves
She stamps your loyalty card

She's a business lady
And good with business men
She's even applied
To go on dragons den

Piccadilly lily
Piccadilly Lily
She drives men silly
Round the streets of Piccadilly

She's an exponent of the genre
A mistress of the art
If you're on the local marathon'
She'll give you a head start

She's a sight to be seen
A challenge to be met

She could even make
Prince Andrew sweat

Take her out to dinner
Take her out to eat
Take her up the Back Street
For a very special treat

She'll have you over starters
She'll have you over mains
The sweetheart of the courses
She never complains

Piccadilly lily
Piccadilly Lily
She drives men silly
Round the streets of Piccadilly

She'll give encouragement
To clients if they're nervous
She's been described as the fourth
Emergency service

She's the real sex queen
Of the northern scene
She's still got it
She's no 'has been

She's out on the street
In all kinds of weather
Her legs are like winter and summer
......Never together

Piccadilly lily
Piccadilly Lily
She drives men silly
Round the streets of Piccadilly

She doesn't want to be hugged
She doesn't want to be kissed
But for a small remuneration
She'll give one off the wrist

She doesn't go for small talk
She thinks there's nothing in it
Besides you're better off
As she charges by the minute

Around the university
Is the best place to be
With student special offer
Buy one get one free

Yes Piccadilly lily
Is the girl that you must see
You'll get a right good sorting
And a painful STD.

Piccadilly lily
Piccadilly Lily
She drives men silly
Round the streets of Piccadilly

On 20th of March 2020 the country went on 'lockdown' because of the Corona Virus. I wrote this on the following Sunday (Mothers Day) We were still in lockdown as this book went to print.

I went for a walk this morning
Early, before most were up
Just me and the sounds of birdsong
And my boots on the cobbles
The odd car in the distance
Someone off to see their mother
A game of Russian roulette
I walked up the local hill
To prove to myself that I could
Occasionally passing a dog walker
With a nod and a half hearted 'hello'
While thinking, keep your distance!
At the top I looked over the valley
There was no sign of panic or of illness, or worry
Just a beautiful landscape
And sheep grazing and feeding their young
All huddled together
They don't know what COVID-19 is
I saw a friend walking the other way
We stopped for a chat, but not close
We would normally have a hug
We don't do that now though
I'll go and walk again tomorrow
If I'm allowed to, if Boris lets me
If not I'll stay in and possibly
Get round to doing stuff I've been putting off
But all of the time, I'll be thinking
Of those at serious risk - maybe even praying
Stay safe

Reviews / Comments

'As with his first book Steve draws on his personal experience and delivers a unique perspective with wit and attitude. Recommended for anyone who has a brain and a heart'.
Henry Normal (Former MD Baby Cow Productions, Poet, writer, producer—The Royal Family, Gavin and Stacey, Mrs. Merton, Alan Partridge etc).

'Arresting engaging poetic verse, laced with class A Northern humour...'
Vinny Peculiar (Musician, songwriter, poet)

'Very well written and a pleasure to read'.
Ian 'POP' Larkin. Salford City Radio

'Most enjoyable. There's a very Northern feel to much of his work'.
'The L.S.Lowry of poetry'
Syd Little (Little & Large)

'His work is refreshingly different and full of humour and pathos. Very well done'.
Mike Lancaster averyfunnyman (Comedian)

'Really great poetry'
George Borowski (Musician / songwriter)

'Funny, poignant and clever'
Linda Jennings (Singer, songwriter, musician)

'Steven's poems possess wit, insight, intelligent observation and social commentary. His recent performance at the famous Cavern Club was a total triumph. Fabulous'!
Nick Bold (Singer songwriter, guitarist 'Virginia Wolfe').

Reviews / Comments

"When he (Steven) asked me to check out this book of his work and give him some feedback. I must say I was astonished and impressed by how carefully crafted these poems are, comedic and serious alike.
As well as being clever and funny, they've also been given that special tender touch. If I wasn't now retired from writing I might even be slightly jealous".
Phil Cool (comedian, writer)

".... a bloody good writer.' When you read a piece and think "Well, that's very true" or "Those are my views exactly" it can be hard to appreciate the work that's gone into it because that's just how YOU would have expressed it. If you could, that is. Have fun reading them - I know I certainly did".
Bernard Wrigley (writer, comedian, poet, actor, musician)

" Steven's poems hold a mirror up to everyday life. They're insightful, thought provoking and funny. And there's more - I defy you not to tap your foot when you're reciting some of them out loud"
Jimmy Cricket (comedian)

"My old mate Steven has written his first book of poetry and it's cracking. Like the secret love child of John Cooper Clarke and Pam Ayres, he muses with warmth and wit on his life, loves and Lancashire. With each verse, the bartender turned tender bard, gradually reveals himself, like his 'girl on the peanut card', and the result is a great read, from a good lad".
Mark Hurst /Mark Miwurdz (comedian, poet, writer)

"A veritable maestro of humourous prose"
Austin Knight (comedian)

".....A funny man and a proper gent who writes proper poems."
Dave Cohen (comedian, writer- Have I Got News For You, Spittin- Image, Horrible Histories)

."..very enjoyable and well written"
Mark Potter (guitarist/writer—Elbow)

Reviews / Comments

*There is a LOT to enjoy and reflect upon in Steven's collection of poems. He seems to have covered just about everything that most people can relate to, laugh at or fear - from the crap on our televisions to preferring to go to North Korea than IKEA; from idiosyncratic British towns with VERY rude names to being unfortunately related to a traffic warden; from the merits of being insignificant to the annoying proliferation of the ubiquitous selfie stick.

Not much escapes his eagle eye and skilful poetic wit – Ryanair; childhood memories; stupid holiday souvenirs; fish and chips; the bland uniformity that blights our towns – you name it he's probably versified about it.

There are also some moving poems about the Manchester arena bombing and some fine tributes to our lovely northern towns.

This book will make you think and make you laugh. I'm pleased to own it and recommend it!

Dave Dutton –(Actor, writer, comic, Lancashire lad).

*Review of 'Reflections'

....'Poetry 'Taylor made' for real people, insightful and delightful'.

John Fleming (Blogger, TV producer, comedy guru).

I love reading the poems Steven writes. every single one either makes me laugh out loud, evokes a memory or poses an interesting question. Often a combination of all the above and more besides to be fair!

Lyndsay Hopkinson (Musician, promoter)

'He takes the everyday and makes it personal and makes you smile'

BBC Radio Lancashire.

'It is always a pleasure to welcome Steven to Bacup Folk Club. His poetry is poignant. funny and always well received. He has a lovely way of viewing the world, with an eye for the real and uniquely absurd. He conveys this in his own inimitable style with rhythm, feeling and integrity'.

Dom Dudill Bacup Folk Club.

Thanks to Dianne Hairsine for this cartoon done during my performance at The Park Inn Swinton on my birthday.

POETRY

Reflections

Top left - Slow Readers Club singer Aaron Starkie. Top right Poet - Tony Walsh. Above - Songwriter / guitarist Aziz Ibrahim.

Legends !
Top left—comedian Phil Cool
Bottom left—Freddie Davis
Right—Syd Little

Above - Poet / TV producer Henry Normal
Below - Inspiral Carpets singer Tom Hingley

In memory of

Alfie Westcott